A WOMAN *of* CONFIDENCE

6 studies for individuals
or groups

Juanita Ryan

Introductions by Linda Shands

With Guidelines for Leaders
and Study Notes

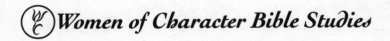 *Women of Character Bible Studies*

InterVarsity Press
Downers Grove, Illinois
Leicester, England

InterVarsity Press
P. O. Box 1400, Downers Grove, IL 60515, USA
38 De Montfort Street, Leicester LE1 7GP, England

InterVarsity Press® is the book-publishing division of InterVarsity Christian Fellowship®, a student
movement active on campus at hundreds of universities, colleges and schools of nursing in the United
States of America, and a member movement of the International Fellowship of Evangelical Students.
For information about local and regional activities, write Public Relations Dept., InterVarsity Christian
Fellowship, 6400 Schroeder Rd., P.O. Box 7895, Madison, WI 53707-7895.

Inter-Varsity Press, UK, is the book-publishing division of the Universities and Colleges Christian
Fellowship (formerly the Inter-Varsity Fellowship), a student movement linking Christian Unions in
universities and colleges throughout the United Kingdom and the Republic of Ireland, and a member
movement of the International Fellowship of Evangelical Students. For information about local and
national activities write to UCCf, 38 De Montfort Street, Leicester LE1 7GP.

USA ISBN 0-8308-2044-2

Printed in the United States of America ∞

Contents

Cast of Characters

Setting the Stage

Each study's introduction takes the perspective of a different character in a continuing story to introduce the theme of each study. Below are the voices behind each introduction.

1 *Sara Moyer* — trapped in an earthquake in California

2 *Hana* — Sara's daughter in Portland, Oregon

3 *Kathy* — Sara's neighbor, also caught in the quake

4 *Beth* — Kathy's mother

5 *Susan* — A rescue worker

6 *Debra* — A Red Cross volunteer

Other characters

Ewock — Sara's dog

Steven — Hana's husband

Mikey — Hana and Steven's son

Rena — Hana and Steven's daughter

Nancy — Hana's friend

Britney — Kathy's daughter

Junior Rylie (J.R.) — a rescue worker, Susan's partner

Introducing *A Woman of Confidence*

My family and I live in earthquake country, so I know what it is to have the ground under my feet suddenly become liquid. It's a strange feeling to lose all confidence that the earth will remain solid and steady, to know that at any minute it might give way. It can leave a person tense and on guard.

Sometimes this is how we feel about trusting God. We are told we can trust him, that his love and power are solid and unshakable. But we may sometimes find ourselves reluctant to place our full confidence in him, fearing that he may fail to respond to us or care for us. As a result, we may live in relationship to God in a tense posture, unable to enjoy the peace that comes from knowing that he is truly rock-solid ground under our feet.

The story which runs through these studies on confidence concerns women who are impacted by a major earthquake. As with any trauma or threat, it is not only their confidence in the earth's solidness that is shaken. Deeper confidences are challenged as well. As we identify with the characters in this story, we can hear them wondering, "Is God here? Does God care?" They call out to God for help. They reach out to each other in love and concern. And they look, in the midst of the trauma, for signs of God's presence and help.

Because we all have times of wondering if God is with us, if he loves us, if he will help us, we all need the gentle reminders and joyful reassurances that the studies in this guide provide. These passages tell us of God's absolute faithfulness to us. The studies offer to strengthen our confidence that God is an "ever-present help in trouble" whom we can be sure of "though the earth give way and the mountains fall into the heart of the sea" (Psalm 46:1-2). These studies take us to rich pastures and still waters where our quiet certainty in God's loving faithfulness can be renewed. May God strengthen your confidence in his unfailing presence and provision in your life as you study his Word of love for you.

Suggestions for Individual Study

1. As you begin each study pray that God will speak to you through his Word.

2. Read the introduction to the study, "Setting the Stage," and respond to the questions that follow it. The story is designed to draw you into the topic at hand and help you begin to see how the Scripture relates to daily life. If there will be a week or more between your studies, then you may want to read all of the introductions in one sitting to get the flow of the ongoing story. This will help if you find that you are having trouble keeping track of all the characters.

3. This is an inductive Bible study, designed to help you discover for yourself what Scripture is saying. Each study deals with a particular passage — so that you can really delve into the author's meaning in that context. Read and reread the passage to be studied. The questions are written using the language of the New International Version, so you may wish to use that version of the Bible. The New Revised Standard Version is also recommended.

4. "God's Word for Us" includes three types of questions. *Observation* questions ask about the basic facts: who, what, when, where and how. *Interpretation* questions delve into the meaning of the passage. *Application* questions (also found in the "Now or Later" section) help you discover the implications of the text for growing in Christ. These three keys unlock the treasures of Scripture.

Write your answers to the study questions in the spaces provided or in a personal journal. Writing can bring clarity and deeper understanding of yourself and of God's Word.

5. Use the study notes at the back of the guide to gain additional insight and information after you have worked through the questions for yourself.

6. Move to the "Now or Later" section. These are ideas for you to freely use in closing your study and responding to God. You may want to choose one of these to do right away and continue working through the other ideas on subsequent days to reinforce what you are learning.

Suggestions for Members of a Group Study

1. Come to the study prepared. Follow the suggestions for individual study mentioned above. You will find that careful preparation will greatly enrich your time spent in group discussion.

2. Be willing to participate in the discussion. The leader of your group will not be lecturing. Instead, she will be encouraging the members of the group to discuss what they have learned. The leader will be asking the questions that are found in this guide.

3. Stick to the topic being discussed. Your answers should be based on the verses which are the focus of the discussion and not on outside authorities such as commentaries or speakers. These studies focus on a particular passage of Scripture. Only rarely should you refer to other portions of the Bible. This allows for everyone to participate on equal ground and for in-depth study.

4. Be sensitive to the other members of the group. Listen attentively when they describe what they have learned. You may be surprised by their insights! Each question assumes a variety of answers. Many questions do not have "right" answers, particularly questions that aim at meaning or application. Instead the questions push us to explore the passage more thoroughly.

When possible, link what you say to the comments of others. Also, be affirming whenever you can. This will encourage some of the more hesitant members of the group to participate.

5. Be careful not to dominate the discussion. We are sometimes so eager to express our thoughts that we leave too little opportunity for others to respond. By all means participate! But allow others to also.

6. Expect God to teach you through the passage being discussed and through the other members of the group. Pray that you will have an enjoyable and profitable time together, but also that as a result of the study, you will find ways that you can take action individually and/or as a group.

7. It will be helpful for groups to follow a few basic

guidelines. These guidelines, which you may wish to adapt to your situation, should be read at the beginning of the first session.

☐ Anything said in the group is considered confidential and will not be discussed outside the group unless specific permission is given to do so.

☐ We will provide time for each person present to talk if he or she feels comfortable doing so.

☐ We will talk about ourselves and our own situations, avoiding conversation about other people.

☐ We will listen attentively to each other.

☐ We will be very cautious about giving advice.

☐ We will pray for each other.

8. If you are the group leader, you will find additional suggestions at the back of the guide.

1

Confidence in God's Unfailing Love For Me

Psalm 33

 Setting the Stage:

Sara's Story

I did think it strange that I hadn't heard the geese. They cross the fields every morning, dark wings drumming, oboe-voices heralding breakfast at my neighbor's pond. Reliable as sunrise.

I stood on our plyboard-covered deck and scanned the eastern sky. A taupe-colored sun had just begun to peek around the crest of Sutter Hill. Nothing. Not even a fly buzzing in the tepid morning air.

Ewock hugged my calf, pointed ears quivering, tail tucked between hind legs. He usually took the three foot leap from the deck to the grass, then raced at warp speed around the yard sounding forth in doggie joy. But not today.

"Go on, Ewock, do your business, I've got to get to work."

He answered with a low growl, then crept, whimpering, back toward the front door.

"Ewock, what's wrong with you?"

A faint thread of music echoed from the windchimes Hana had given me for Mother's Day. Their jingle turned to a clatter as the ground rolled, then jerked me off my feet and threw me face down onto the wooden deck.

Quake! The thought had barely registered when the boards beneath me gave way. I heard a crack, like someone splitting wood, then dawn went crashing into night.

Silence. Darkness—absolute. First thought: *I must be dead.* Face down. Lying flat. Pressure on my chest and back. *Breathe.* Choking on dirt. *Spit.* Then move my head to the side and try again. Better; warm and stagnant, but it's air.

Alive. *Lie still and listen for the pain.* Nothing. Just an unrelenting pressure on my upper body. I work both arms, both legs. They will move every way but up. *Dig in elbows, try to slither forward.* Pain! Sharp and strong and black.

Awake again. Somehow I know it's cooler out there. *How long have I been trapped? an hour? a day? I won't try to move—once burned twice shy.* I chuckle, but it comes out sounding like a moan. *Shh.* Nails skittering on wood. "Ewock?" *Don't whisper—shout!*

Pain sears my lungs as I try to draw a deeper breath. "Ewock. Here boy, come."

I've no idea what I think he can do, but the relief I feel when I hear his panting breath is total. His slobbery tongue across my cheek is ecstacy. He curls up by my head, chin nestled on my hair.

"No, boy. Go. Get some help." I dig my fingers under his ribs until he moves, scrambling forward. I tip my head back, following his progress. Light. Above and in front of me. *He must have dug a hole in the rubble.*

It's tempting to try once more. *Slide easy toward the light.* This time I see red instead of black. *Please, God.*

Lie still and fight. Open your eyes. Yell.

Not enough breath. My mouth is dry as chalk. I close my eyes again and hear a whirling chopping sound. Damp wind swirls through the hole that Ewock made. I turn my face into my armpit trying to avoid the dust. *Dear Lord . . .*

The clamor rises, swirls to a raging din. Hovering, I'm convinced, just inches above my head. *Oh, Lord, my God . . .*

The wood above me vibrates as the chopper pulls away. I tense, waiting for the crushing blow. Instead, the pressure lifts, minutely, but I can move a little easier. I stretch toward the light. *Ignore the pain.* My fingers grip the edge of the hole. Ewock barking, running in circles, saliva dripping on my skin.

Jesus loves me, this I know . . .

---

1. There can be an interactive effect between our level of confidence in God's love and how we perceive and respond to life's events. As you reflect on Sara's experience, how might her confidence in God's love for her affect her in this time of distress?

How might the earthquake and her injury impact her confidence in God's love for her?

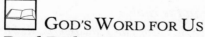

GOD'S WORD FOR US
Read Psalm 33.

2. The psalmist begins by telling us to "praise the LORD."

What does he suggest we do to praise God (vv. 1-3)?

What other activities might you add to this list?

_____

3. Restate in your own words the reason the psalmist gives for this praise (vv. 4-5).

_____

4. What response do you have to God's powerful acts which are described in verses 6-11?

_____

5. What do these opening verses (4-11) tell us about God?

How might this build a person's confidence in God's love?

6. Verses 12-19 present a contrast—or a choice—of placing our confidence in our strength or putting our confidence in God's love. What does the Scripture say about these two choices?

_____

7. What personal qualities do you see as "strengths" that you might be inclined to trust in place of trusting God's love for you?

_____

8. Verses 20-21 describe the people's response to God's unfailing love. List the three responses.

How might having a solid confidence in God's unfailing love for you help you to respond in these ways?

9. What makes it difficult for you to experience confidence in God's unfailing love for you?

What increases your confidence in God's unfailing love for you?

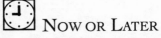 NOW OR LATER

☐ The final verse is a prayer that God's unfailing love will "rest upon us . . . as we put our hope [confidence] in you." What pictures come to mind as you read these words? Spend time journaling your response. Reflect on your thoughts and feelings in response to this prayer.

☐ Make the prayer of the last verse your own, expanding it to the specific needs you have right now.

☐ How might the responses of verses 20-21 (waiting for God with hope, joy and trust) become practical, everyday realities for you? Think of one or two simple activities you might do to increase your hope, joy and trust. Practice these activities all week. Take note of the results in you.

☐ Read Romans 8:31-39.

2

....

Confidence in God's Power and Presence with Me

Psalm 99

 SETTING THE STAGE:

Hana's Story

After I finished cutting up Mikey's french toast, I grabbed the phone on the sixth ring.

"Hana, I'm sorry to call so early, but I just heard the news. Is your mom okay?"

"Why?" My heart raced at the panic in her voice. "I just talked to her last night, she's fine."

My friend's silence scared me worse than her words. "Nancy? What's going on?"

"Oh, Hana, I'm so sorry. There's been a quake. A seven pointer. And the epicenter was in Clarkston. You'd better turn on the news."

The small TV was on the counter. I grabbed the remote and switched from cartoons to CNN.

"...a breach in the Clarkston Dam has poured thousands of gallons of water onto the already devastated countryside. Searchers continue to comb the rural area for survivors, but are hindered by the flooding and mountainous terrain."

I stared at the choppy footage: Fractured trees scattered like toothpicks, flattened houses, a sea of muddy water where the fields should be. . . . Somewhere in that unrecognizable mess was my childhood home.

"Hana? . . . Hana!" Nancy's shout shook me from my stupor.

Mom. My face and hands felt clammy and my stomach churned. "What am I going to do, Nancy? I . . . I don't . . . What should I do?"

She drew a sharp breath and let it out again. "Okay. First, where are the kids?"

I shuddered and looked down into two puzzled faces staring up at me. "Wrong, Mama?" Rena's syrup-sticky mouth was puckered and Mikey's eyes were huge with fear.

I sat, tucked the phone under my chin, and pulled them both into my lap. "They're right here." *Safe.*

"Good. I'll get a prayer chain going and be there in twenty minutes."

She made the drive in half that time and her hug was like a life-line.

We called the Red Cross. After six tries, I finally got a message machine telling me all lines were busy. Then we called Steven at his hotel in Tokyo, but it would be hours before he got the message and at least two days before he could get home to take care of our kids.

"I can't just sit here; I have to do something."

"Wait." Nancy pointed the remote at the TV and turned up the volume. "Listen."

". . . rescue efforts continue. All phone lines are down and airports as far away as San Francisco are closed. Red Cross volunteers are being flown in to Los Angeles and bused to the area. People seeking information about loved ones are being asked to call one of the following numbers . . ."

No Sara Moyer on any of the lists. "They're just begin-ning to bring in survivors from the outlying areas." The voice sounded tired, but sympathetic. "Try again in a couple of hours."

Nancy wrapped her arms around me and, for the fifth time that morning, we prayed. Or rather, she did. *Please, God*, was the only prayer my rattled thoughts would form.

At noon Nancy opened a can of soup. "You have to eat something." But my stomach cringed at the thought of food.

I put the kids down for a nap. A little hand escaped the covers and Mikey, his blue eyes dark with worry, patted my cheek. "It okay, Mama?" I wrapped him in a hug and then rescued his teddy bear from the old suitcase we had given him to play with.

Go. The thought echoed as though it were spoken out loud. *Fly to LA, then the bus, then walk if I have to, but go.*

I looked into my son's beseeching eyes and handed him the bear. "Yes, baby, God loves you, it's going to be okay."

I felt calm and strong. And very, very right.

---

1. As Hana moved through this frightening day, how did God demonstrate his presence with her?

What thoughts and feelings do you have as you reflect on the ways Hana and Nancy relied on God's power and presence?

Recall a time when you especially needed to rely on God's power and presence. What happened?

 GOD'S WORD FOR US

Read Psalm 99.

2. What pictures come to mind as you read verses 1-2?

3. Why is it significant that God, who is "exalted over all the nations," loves justice and equity (vv. 3-4)?

4. What do you learn about his relationship with Moses and Aaron and with Israel (vv. 6-8)?

What do you learn from this about God's involvement with us?

5. This psalm declares three different times (vv. 3, 5 and 9) that the Lord "is holy." Before making this declaration, these verses describe God in striking language that tell us something of what it means that God is holy. List what is said about God in these verses.

What does this tell you about what it means that God is holy?

——————————————————————

6. According to this psalm, how are we to respond to God's holiness, power and presence in our lives?

——————————————————————

7. What do you experience as you reflect on God's power?

What do you experience as you reflect on God's presence in your life?

8. What difference would it make to you if you were able to experience greater confidence in God's power?

What difference would it make to you if you were able to experience greater confidence in God's presence in your life?

 NOW OR LATER

☐ Make a list of some of the things you do not have power over in your life, but which concern you. Allow yourself to release these things and your anxieties over them to God.

☐ Write a brief prayer, thanking God for some of the ways his power and presence are evident in your life.

☐ Read Psalm 18.

3

Confidence in God's Provision for Me

Psalm 107

 SETTING THE STAGE:

Kathy's Story

The geese didn't show. I scattered their breakfast in the chicken yard, but not one hen would leave the roost. I heard our Guernseys milling around the barn, lowing piteously and felt the first pinprick of fear.

You don't live in quake country long without learning to read the signs. The animals know what's coming long before we do. I scanned the horizon. Not a cloud in sight. The tops of the trees stood petrified; still. They talk about the calm before the storm, but I knew in my bones this storm would have nothing to do with the weather.

Britney and Mom! When I'd come outside they'd been at the kitchen table, Mom cradling her second cup of coffee, Brit scarfing down a bowl of cereal and cramming for a test on fractions. I dropped the feed bucket and ran.

I almost made it. The first roll threw me off balance. The second, like a giant hand, scooped me up and flung me backwards. I couldn't breathe. The hand had no mercy, jolting, jerking, banging my head against the ground.

When it finally stopped, I stared up into the branches of our huge red maple and felt water soaking through my jeans. I wrapped my arms around the trunk; solid, unbending, then stood and clung to it waiting for the roaring in my ears to cease.

The dam! The thought was like a slap to my sluggish mind. I jerked my eyes toward the small concrete structure less than a mile away. Muddy water spewed over the spillway into the already swollen river.

I lift up my eyes to the hills. Where does my help come from? As a child I could have quoted the entire psalm. Now, I was grateful for the scrap of memory. *Mom and Britney.* We had to get to higher ground.

I nearly lost it when I saw the house, a pile of glass and rubble where the kitchen should have been. *They cannot be alive.* My mother and ten-year-old daughter could not possibly have survived in there.

The water had risen half way to my knees. "Mom! Britney!" *Lord God help me find them!* I dug at a pile of shakes that used to be our roof. It wouldn't budge. I moved on around the house, calling, then listening, searching for a way in — or out. *Please God, help me get them out.*

Finally, around the corner from the kitchen, where the mudroom should have been, I discovered a small opening guarded by a copper pipe. Water was already seeping in. I put my mouth close to the hole and hollered like a branded steer. *"Mother!"*

"Mama?"

My daughter's cry was punch-in-the-stomach relief. When I caught my breath, I tore at the plasterboard and yelled some more. "This way, Britney. Can you move?

Come this way."

I bent down and peered around the pipe. They were crawling on their bellies, sliding forward inch by inch, Mom's voice, steady, calming, urging Britney on. "Almost there, baby. Keep on moving. You're doing fine."

I tore upward at the plaster. Britney could get through, but what about Mom? Kneeling in water to my waist, I wrapped both hands around the pipe and gave a final heave. It bent. Not much, but enough.

Britney was choking. *Help us, God. Don't let me lose them now!*

I reached in blind, grabbed the shoulders of my daughter's denim jumper and hauled her out. "Stand up! Stay above the water line." Then my mother. Up and out, Britney's small hands guiding, tugging just above my own.

The water was rising fast. There was no time to find out where the blood on Britney's face was coming from. We had to get to higher ground. "Hold on." I shouted even though they were right next to me. As their hands gripped mine, I turned toward the hills.

---

1. How might Kathy's actions offer us a picture of the help God provides for us in times of need?

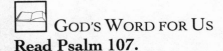 GOD'S WORD FOR US
Read Psalm 107.

2. This psalm describes a variety of situations in which people are in need of help. List the situations which are described (leave the second column blank).

Situations of Need   **God's Response**

3. Which of these situations do you think Kathy, her daughter and her mother might most identify with? Explain.

Which of these situations do you most identify with? Explain.

4. Now go back to your list of situations and describe the ways God responds to the people experiencing these various needs.

5. What do God's responses tell us about God?

6. A theme in these situations is that when the people call out to God for help, God responds. Why is it important to ask for God's help?

---

7. How does the psalmist suggest we respond to God when we receive his help?

---

8. The last verse of the psalm says "whoever is wise, let him heed these things." What wisdom does this psalm offer?

---

9. The last verse also says "whoever is wise, let him . . . consider the great love of the LORD." What impact does it have on your thoughts, feelings, beliefs and behaviors when you consider the great love of the Lord for you?

 NOW OR LATER

☐ Spend some time thanking God for the help he has provided you throughout your life.

☐ Spend some time asking God for the help you need at this time in your life.

☐ Read Matthew 6:25-34.

4

....

Confidence in God's Care for Me

Psalm 16

 SETTING THE STAGE:

Beth's Story

That dining room set was made from solid oak. By my
Henry's own hands, God bless him. If it hadn't been for
that table . . .

I'll never forget the noise; like an Air Force jet was
landing on the roof. Then I looked up at the chandelier.

Britney must have seen it too. "Earthquake, Grandma,"
she hollered, then ducked under the table like they taught
her in school.

I landed next to her and tried to shield her body with mine.
The floor bucked and rolled, jerking us around like old rag
dolls. When it settled, the silence was worse than the roar.

Britney wiggled out from underneath me. She was
bleeding some and plenty scared. When I tried to move,
pain stabbed like white lightning through my arm. I
sucked in air and closed my eyes.

"Grandma?"

Don't panic, you've got to get her out of here. "Grandma's here, baby. It's okay." *Please, God.*

What a mess. All around us, heaps of plaster, wood and broken glass. Which way was out?

Britney still had on one shoe. Where the other went, I couldn't guess. "Try pushing with your foot." My slippers were no good, but she pushed and dug, and I helped her with my one good arm. Finally I saw a speck of light and heard Kathy's voice.

His sheep know his voice . . . He leads them out.

Later, from the top of the hill I could see how the roof had fallen at an angle creating a tunnel for us to crawl through.

The barn was gone and water covered the fields. Houses, cars, rooted up trees — the river wasn't partial to what it took. A dead cow swept by. I turned away and focused on Britney, keeping pressure on the cut above her eye, while her mother huddled close to keep her warm.

My shoulder was broken for sure, but no need to tell them yet. Wouldn't do a speck of good for Kath to worry more.

We heard the helicopter long before we saw it. It circled us once, then flew on up over the dam.

"What's wrong with them, can't they see us?" Kathy jumped up and down waving her arms.

"They saw us, honey. They're searching for survivors. I'm sure they can't set down in this flood. They'll have a better chance above the dam."

We watched the chopper disappear behind some trees. The engine tone changed and I knew it must have landed in a pasture. "That would be Sara Moyer's house. I hope she's okay."

The chopper took off again, circling the farms up along

London Road. I calculated just about half an hour before they headed back our way. This time they hovered long enough to drop a parcel practically right into our laps. Kathy scrambled to retrieve it: Blankets, apples, trail mix, a first aid kit and six small pouches of juice.

"Looks like we might be here awhile." I hadn't meant to say it out loud. My shoulder throbbed. The cut on Britney's head had stopped bleeding, but Kathy's eyes had taken on a glassy look.

Britney grabbed the trail mix and opened the juice. "How long, Grandma? What should we do while we wait?" She looked at me and grinned. "Besides pray, I mean."

I smiled back at her. "Let's sing. You choose first."

Her little voice rang pure and sweet, "Praise God from whom all blessings flow . . . " I added my contralto, then Kathy straightened her shoulders and joined in like it was the most natural thing in all the world.

---

1. After the shock wears off, and these three women reflect on this day, what evidence of God's care are they likely to see?

---

2. Psalm 16 begins by asking God for protection, for refuge: "Keep me safe, O God, for in you I take refuge." After this day, what images might come to Beth's mind when she thinks about a refuge?

When you think of God as a refuge, what picture comes to mind?

 GOD'S WORD FOR US
Read Psalm 16.

3. The statements in verses 2 and 3 stand in contrast to the statements in verse 4. What contrast is being made?

4. What gifts of care does the psalmist say God has provided in verses 5-11?

5. How does the psalmist respond to God's care?

6. Make a list of some of the gifts of care God has provided for you.

7. What thoughts and feelings do you have in response to these gifts of care from God?

8. What fears and doubts might hamper Kathy's, Britney's and Beth's confidence in God's care after this day?

What fears and doubts hamper your confidence in God's care for you?

9. Verse 9 states "my body also will rest secure." The psalmist is expressing a deep confidence in God's care. What might help Kathy, Britney and Beth experience confidence in God's care, so their traumatized bodies can rest secure?

What helps you experience confidence in God's care for you?

NOW OR LATER

☐ Picture your body resting secure. Take some time to relax and let your body rest. See yourself resting in God's arms, or in a place of beauty God has provided for you. Picture yourself at peace because you are sure of God's ongoing care for you.

☐ Keeping a log or journal of God's gifts to you might help you build your confidence in God's ongoing care for you. Try doing this for a week. Share your entries with a friend.

☐ Read Psalm 142.

5

....

Confidence in God's Work in My Life

Psalm 25

 SETTING THE STAGE:

Susan's Story

The hardest part was having to leave people behind. Stranded on hills and rooftops; anything solid, they stayed. The most we could do was throw them blankets and a little food. *They're the lucky ones*, I reminded myself as we flew over another flattened farm house.

Six a.m. People had been sleeping, shaving, eating breakfast, doing morning chores. Now they were buried under the rubble of their own homes and barns. "How many," I wondered aloud, "are still alive?"

Junior Rylie patted my hand. "That's what we're here to find out."

I forced a smile, glad I'd drawn J.R. as a partner. He was fiftyish, but strong and smart. A Vietnam vet. He'd probably seen worse than this. Not me. Two years as a paramedic, I'd seen some nasty accidents, but nothing like this. Natural disaster. A disaster all right, but I couldn't see anything natural about it.

"Over there!" The pilot circled lower, and I followed his pointing arm. A little dog bouncing and running in circles on what looked like a plywood dance floor. "Let's drop in for a closer look."

We hovered as close as we dared, but even the noise and wind from the chopper blades did not deter the dog.

I focused on the object of his attention. *A hand. Movement.* J.R. hollered. "We got a live one, Charlie. Set us down."

The nearest open ground was a pasture about a quarter mile away. *Me, J.R. and the radio,* I thought, *all the hope that person has.* But even as we picked our way around cracks and fissures and over fallen trees, I knew that wasn't true. *It's hard to see you in this God,* I prayed, *but I know you're here.*

A tremor sent us scrambling for hand holds above the crumbling dirt. I wrapped my arms around the trunk of a huge Douglas Fir, but it was already over.

"Just a jiggle." J.R's smile was reassuring. "Let's hope it didn't do more damage to our patient."

I grabbed the medical bag and pushed ahead. Stay clear of fallen telephone wires. Farm fencing. Cut our way through. The little dog barked louder, getting more and more excited as we drew near.

We ran the last twenty yards. The dog backed away and lay down, drooling, panting, obviously exhausted.

"Pick-up sticks. This won't be easy."

I nodded, lay down on my belly and stretched my arm across the platform—a patio roof?—circled my fingers around a woman's slender wrist, found a pulse.

"What's that humming sound? Does she have a radio down there?"

I inched forward, praying that the board wouldn't shift and shined my flashlight past the hand suspended from the hole. Her face turned toward me, eyes closed, a bloody scrape across her cheek, her throat emitting tuneless words; faint and thready as her pulse. My eyes flooded. *Jesus Loves Me.*

"What?"

"She's singing, J.R."

"Conscious then?"

"Barely. Shock, for sure." My flashlight played across the rubble. "A beam across her upper back. Not crushing her though."

"Not yet." He lifted the radio and spoke to ground control.

I reached down and brushed the sticky hair back off her forehead. *Shine the penlight in one eye. Pass on the stats. Start I.V. Check the bag for morphine. She'll need it when we move that beam. Wait for more help to come.* I held her hand and rested my cheek against the boards. *Keep singing, lady,* I wanted to tell her. *You keep singing and we'll be okay.*

---

1. In Psalm 25 the psalmist asks to be released from a snare. Sara was literally caught in a snare. How do you see God working in Sara's life?

---

2. What might it have meant to Susan to trust God in her situation—in practical terms?

What does this mean in practical terms to you?

GOD'S WORD FOR US
Read Psalm 25.

3. The psalmist asks God to work in his life. List the requests the psalmist makes of God in verses 1-7.

4. What does the psalmist appeal to as he makes these requests?

5. Verses 8-14 offer several insights into God's work in our lives. What kind of work does the psalmist say God will do in our lives?

6. In verses 15-22 the psalmist describes the distress he is experiencing. What does he say about his distress?

7. What work does he ask God to do on his behalf in this time of distress?

8. Which of these requests might Susan or Sara have been making of God?

Which of these requests do you echo at this time in your life?

---

9. What evidence is there in your life that God has been and is at work?

How does this evidence affect your level of confidence in God's work in your life?

 NOW OR LATER

☐ List all the attributes of God named in this psalm. Focus on one or two of these truths about God this week.

☐ What work are you aware of needing God to do? Write to God about the work you are needing and willing for him to do in your life.

☐ Read 1 Corinthians 12.

6

....

Confidence in Who God Made Me to Be

Ephesians 2:1-10

 SETTING THE STAGE:

Debra's Story

Wrinkled clothing, stringy uncombed hair, a ratty suitcase clutched in a white knuckled fist. *Another refugee.* I turned my attention back to the line. I'd been handing out water in plastic gallon jugs for two hours now and my back was beginning to ache.

She pushed in front of me. "I'm looking for my mother."

"Is she a volunteer?" I passed a bottle to the grumbling man behind her and reached for another, but she grabbed my arm.

"Please. I've been looking for two days."

The line behind her shifted and stirred. "Come on, lady, move it." . . . "Yeah, wait your turn."

I looked into the woman's eyes. Exhausted, desperate, determined. Not violent. Why had she singled me out?

I beckoned a fellow Red Cross volunteer. "I could use a break. Would you please take over for awhile?"

I led the woman to a group of folding chairs and eased her down. Was she in shock? No blood or bruises. No apparent broken bones. *Take it slowly, gently.* "What's your name?"

"Hana. My mother's name is Sara. I grew up here."

"Well, Hana, when did you last see your mother?"

Her brow wrinkled. "Uh, about three months ago, I guess." She flicked a strand of hair out of her face, like swatting a fly.

"Why is that important? I need to find her now. She was in the quake. One mile up. Above the Clarkston Dam."

The light dawned. "Where do you live now, Hana?"

"Portland. Oregon, not Maine." Her eyes teared. "Why won't someone help me?"

How in the world had she gotten here? Transportation routes were still closed to anything but emergency vehicles. We had come in with the National Guard.

"The lists are in the office next door." *Right next to the makeshift hospital and morgue.* I shuddered. *Lord, you have to help me.* How could I tell this women her mother was probably dead, her body still buried under tons of debris?

I led her through the sea of bruised and broken flesh. *So much suffering.* The office door was locked. BACK IN FIFTEEN MINUTES. One of the nurses lay a sympathetic hand on my shoulder, "Put her over there." She nodded at a vacant cot.

I didn't bother to explain. Hana's feet were swollen twice their size. She needed rest as much as anyone here.

"Hana? Hana Moyer?"

"Kathy? Oh, Kath, you made it." The two women hugged and Hana came alive. "I thought . . . the dam and all. What about . . .?"

"They're okay. Britney got away with twenty stitches

and a goose egg. Mother has a broken collarbone. I'm surprised you didn't see her, she's right over there next to your mom."

Alive then. Praise God. I turned to go, but another hand gripped my arm.

"Please, you have to help me. My son . . . " The boy she carried was pale, bleeding from an already bandaged head wound. I led them to the vacant cot.

A nurse handed me a stack of gauze pads. "Hold this while I take a look." I followed her instructions as she cleaned and rebandaged the wound.

"I'm not supposed to be here," I said. "I belong next door." But the nurse had moved on.

A doctor in paper-covered shoes and a blood-stained scrub jacket stopped and peered at my nametag. "Debra, is it? Let's get those cots made up, we've got a new batch of wounded coming in."

Serve where you're planted. I bit off my protest and did as I was told.

---

1. What work had God prepared for Debra to do?

[ ] GOD'S WORD FOR US

Read Ephesians 2:1-10 as if it was written personally to you.

2. What does the text tell you about who you are?

3. What thoughts and feelings do you have about this description of yourself?

4. Which part of this description do you relate to the most easily?

Which part is the most difficult for you to relate to?

5. What does the text tell you about God's relationship with you?

6. What does the text tell you about what God wants to give you?

7. What is our part in all of this, according to the text?

8. What work are you aware of that God has prepared for you to do?

_____

9. How does this text help increase your confidence in who God made you to be?

 NOW OR LATER

☐ Write a character sketch of yourself, as if you were a character in a novel.

☐ Write a prayer to God, thanking him for who he made you to be.

☐ Read Psalm 8.

Guidelines for Leaders

My grace is sufficient for you. (2 Corinthians 12:9)

If leading a Bible study is something new for you, don't worry. These studies are designed to be led easily. As a matter of fact, the flow of questions through the passage from observation to interpretation to application is so natural that you may feel that the studies lead themselves.

You don't need to be an expert on the Bible or a trained teacher to lead a Bible discussion. The idea behind these inductive studies is that the leader guides group members to discover for themselves what the Bible has to say. This method of learning will allow group members to remember much more of what is said than a lecture would.

This study guide is flexible. You can use it with a variety of groups — student, professional, neighborhood or church groups. Each study takes about forty-five minutes in a group setting with the possibility of extending the time to sixty minutes or more by adding questions from "Now or Later."

There are some important facts to know about group dynamics and encouraging discussion. The suggestions listed below should enable you to effectively and enjoyably fulfill your role as leader.

Preparing for the Study

1. Ask God to help you understand and apply the passage in your own life. Unless this happens, you will not be prepared to lead others. Pray too for the various members of the group. Ask God to open your hearts to the message of his Word and motivate you to action.

2. Read the introduction to the entire guide to get an overview of the subject at hand and the issues which will be explored. Also read through the introductions to each study to get the flow of the continuing story that runs through the guide and to get familiar with the characters. Be ready to refer the group to the list of characters on the back of the contents page if they have questions about the story.

3. As you begin each study, read and reread the assigned Bible passage to familiarize yourself with it.

4. This study guide is based on the New International Version of the Bible. It will help you and the group if you use this translation as the basis for your study and discussion.

5. Carefully work through each question in the study. Spend time in meditation and reflection as you consider how to respond.

6. Write your thoughts and responses in the space provided in the study guide. This will help you to express your understanding of the passage clearly.

7. It might help you to have a Bible dictionary handy. Use it to look up any unfamiliar words, names or places. (For additional help on how to study a passage, see chapter five of *Leading Bible Discussions*, InterVarsity Press.)

8. Take the "Now or Later" portion of each study seriously. Consider how you need to apply the Scripture to your life. Remember that the group will follow your lead in responding to the studies. They will not go any deeper than you do.

Leading the Study

1. Begin the study on time. Open with prayer, asking God to help the group to understand and apply the passage.

2. Be sure that everyone in your group has a study guide. Encourage the group to prepare beforehand for each discussion by reading the introduction to the guide and by working through the questions in the study.

3. At the beginning of your first time together, explain that these studies are meant to be discussions, not lectures. Encourage the members of the group to participate. However, do not put pressure on those who may be hesitant to speak during the first few sessions.

4. Have a group member read the story in "Setting the Stage" at the beginning of the discussion or allow group members some time to read this silently. These stories are designed to draw the readers into the topic of the study and show how the topic is related to our daily lives. It is merely a starting point so don't allow the group members to get bogged down with details of the story or with trying to make a literal connection to the passage to be studied. Just enjoy them.

5. Every study begins with one or more "approach" questions, which are meant to be asked before the passage is read. These questions are designed to connect the opening story with the theme of the study and to encourage group members to begin to open up. Encourage as many members as possible to participate and be ready to get the discussion going with your own response.

Approach questions can reveal where our thoughts or feelings need to be transformed by Scripture. That is why it is especially important not to read the passage before the approach question is asked. The passage will tend to color the honest reactions people would otherwise give because they are, of course, supposed to think the way the Bible does.

6. Have a group member read aloud the passage to be studied.

7. As you ask the questions under "God's Word for Us," keep in mind that they are designed to be used just as they are written. You may simply read them aloud. Or you may prefer to express them in your own words.

There may be times when it is appropriate to deviate from the study guide. For example, a question may have already been answered. If so, move on to the next question. Or someone may raise an important question not covered in the guide. Take time to discuss it, but try to keep the group from going off on tangents.

8. Avoid answering your own questions. If necessary, repeat or rephrase them until they are clearly understood. An eager group quickly becomes passive and silent if they think the leader will do most of the talking.

9. Don't be afraid of silence. People may need time to think about the question before formulating their answers.

10. Don't be content with just one answer. Ask, "What do the rest of you think?" or "anything else?" until several people have given answers to the question.

11. Acknowledge all contributions. Try to be affirming whenever possible. Never reject an answer. If it is clearly off-base, ask, "Which verse led you to that conclusion?" or again, "What do the rest of you think?"

12. Don't expect every answer to be addressed to you,

even though this will probably happen at first. As group members become more at ease, they will begin to truly interact with each other. This is one sign of healthy discussion.

13. Don't be afraid of controversy. It can be very stimulating. If you don't resolve an issue completely, don't be frustrated. Move on and keep it in mind for later. A subsequent study may solve the problem.

14. Periodically summarize what the group has said about the passage. This helps to draw together the various ideas mentioned and gives continuity to the study. But don't preach.

15. "Now or Later" can be used in a variety of ways depending on the time available to you and the interests of your group members. You may want to discuss an application question or idea and make some commitments. Or you may want to allow five minutes or so of quiet reflection within the group time so that people can journal their responses. Then, ask simply, "What did you experience (and/or learn) as you journaled?"

You will want to use at least one of these ideas to wrap up the group time, but you may want to encourage group members to continue working through other ideas throughout the week. You can continue discussing what has been learned at your next meeting.

16. Conclude your time together with conversational prayer. Ask for God in following through on the commitments you've made.

17. End on time.

Many more suggestions and helps are found in *Small Group Leaders' Handbook* and *The Big Book on Small Groups* (both from InterVarsity Press). Reading through one of these books would be worth your time.

Study Notes

Study 1. Confidence in God's Unfailing Love for Me. Psalm 33.

Purpose: To build confidence in God's love for us.

Question 2. The psalmist calls us to sing, make music on instruments, and shout for joy in order to express our praise to God for who he is. You may be familiar or unfamiliar with these expressions of joy and praise. You may feel comfortable or uncomfortable with them.

If you are leading a group, encourage discussion about the benefits of expressing joy in such open ways and about what inhibits us from expressing joy this openly. Encourage group members to talk about other ways they find themselves expressing joy and praise to God.

Question 3. The reasons the psalmist gives for this joy and praise have to do with who God is. God is faithful in all he does, his word is trustworthy, he loves righteousness and justice, and his unfailing love fills the earth.

Question 4. If you are leading a group, encourage discussion about who God is according to verses 6-11. Participants may have different responses to these pictures of God's power. Some may feel awe and joy, others might feel fear.

Question 5. It is important to put together the entire picture the psalmist is presenting about God. He is showing us that God is good and infinitely loving and all powerful. He is showing us that God is the Creator and that his unfailing love is with all he has made.

Question 6. The contrast is between trusting in the things that make us feel strong and secure by our own efforts (in this case, weapons of war—armies, horses) and trusting in God's unfailing love. Identify a variety of things you trust in that make you feel strong and secure, such as intelligence, common sense, hard work, the (seeming) ability to take care of things by yourself. All of these things are "vain hope." That is, they are illusions. They do not save us, because we cannot save ourselves. We are daily, hourly dependent on God's unfailing love.

Question 8. The responses of the people to God's unfailing love which are listed in verses 20-21 are: (1) waiting in hope, (2) rejoicing in God and (3) trusting his holy name. Consider in practical terms what each of these means in your life.

It is difficult to wait with hope or feel joy or trust in God when our confidence in his love is at a low point. When our confidence in God's love is strong, it is much easier to anticipate that he will see us through a difficult time. It is natural to feel joy, and trust is made possible.

Question 9. Group members will have a wide variety of experiences to share about what builds their confidence in God's love and what makes it difficult to experience this confidence. If you are leading, encourage the group to think about times when their confidence was strong and times when it was shaken. What were the contributing factors?

Now or Later. The prayer that God's unfailing love will rest on us is a prayer of blessing. It is a request that God will show us his love, touch us with his love, build our trust and confidence in his love. Our confidence in God's love often comes as a gift from God's Spirit.

Study 2. Confidence in God's Power and Presence with Me. Psalm 99.

Purpose: To increase confidence in God's power and presence in our lives.

Question 2. The opening verses of this psalm present powerful pictures of God as Ruler and King of all the earth. Describe what you "see" as you read these verses.

Question 3. It is important to realize that God is not only Ruler and King of all the earth, but that he is not a tyrant. He loves all of us. He wants each of us to be treated with respect and fairness. He loves fairness. He loves justice. He is not the kind of ruler who accepts bribes (or campaign donations) from powerful people who make money in ways that are hurtful to others. He is not the kind of ruler who plays favorites. He does not cater to the rich or powerful or beautiful. He loves the poor and the powerless and the plain-looking among us, and he loves us deeply. He does not want any of his children treated with anything but justice, fairness, respect and love.

Question 4. This psalm teaches us that God is deeply involved with us. He knows us by name. He knows us individually (Moses, Aaron, Samuel). He answers us when we call to him. He forgives us, he corrects our misdeeds, he gives us guidance in his statutes and decrees.

Question 5. These verses tell us that God is "great,"

"exalted over all the nations," "awesome" and "mighty." According to *The New Bible Dictionary:*

> Holiness in the OldTestament as in the New Testament is applied in the highest sense to God. It denotes . . . the transcendence of God. . . . The word also denotes relationship, and signifies God's determination to preserve His own position relative to all other free beings. . . . Not only does it bring out the contrast between the divine and the human, but it becomes almost synonymous with supreme deity, and emphasizes, in particular, the awe-inspiring side of the divine character.
>
> The ethical quality in holiness is, however, the aspect under which the term is applied most commonly to God. Holiness is a term for the moral excellence of God and His freedom from all limitation in His moral perfection. . . . Since holiness embraces every distinctive attribute of Godhead, it may be defined as the outshining of all that God is. (J. D. Douglas, ed. [Grand Rapids, Mich.: Eerdmans, 1971], p. 530)

Question 6. The response this psalm calls for to God's power and presence in our lives is to praise God, to exalt him, to worship him. It is a response of giving our attention to God, acknowledging our dependence on him, acknowledging who he is, rejoicing in his goodness and care.

Question 7. You may respond to thoughts about God's power with awe and joy and gratitude. Or you may respond with fear, or with a mixture of these feelings.

You may respond to God's presence in your life with belief or disbelief, hope, relief, trust or uncertainty. If you are leading, encourage the group to share whatever responses they may have.

Question 8. As you reflect on the difference it might make to experience greater confidence in God's power, if you are leading a group, you might find it useful to have members think about problems and difficulties they face in the present.

Awareness and confidence in God's personal love and care and involvement in our lives can make all the difference in the degree of peace we feel. It means we are not forgotten. It means that God is paying attention. It means that God cares. It means that the events in our lives have purpose, even when that purpose is hidden from us.

Study 3. Confidence in God's Provision for Me. Psalm 107.

Purpose: To grow in confidence of God's help in our lives.

Question 2. In this question focus on the situations. We'll come back to God's responses. The situations people find themselves faced with in this psalm include: (1) being caught in the hand of an enemy (vv. 2-3), (2) wandering homeless, hungry, thirsty, with their lives ebbing away (vv. 4-5), (3) sitting in darkness and deepest gloom, in prison, in chains, rebelling against God, bitterly laboring (vv. 10-12), (4) suffering illness (because of sin), so that they were not able to eat and were dying (vv. 17-18), (5) being threatened by an enormous storm at sea so that all courage melted away (vv. 23-27), (6) being hungry in a desert that would yield nothing (and also being oppressed by foes) (vv. 33-39).

Question 3. If you are struggling with parallels to your life, look at these situations metaphorically. You may not be experiencing these physical problems but these situations may depict your emotional or spiritual state.

Question 4. God responds by helping the people in these situations by: (1) delivering us from the hand of our foes, (2) satisfying our hunger and thirst and our need for a place to live and to belong, (3) breaking our chains and bringing us out of darkness, (4) healing us and restoring our lives, (5) quieting the storm, (6) turning rivers into desert to stop the wicked and turning the desert into fruitful land.

Question 5. The psalm tells us that these things teach us about God's goodness and great love for us. The psalm shows us God's power, his involvement, his attention, his responsiveness, his love. It show us that God is willing and ready to answer our calls for help.

Question 6. It is important to ask for God's help, not because God doesn't know we need help unless we ask, but because *we* don't know we need help. We think we are suppose to do things on our own, or that we are better if we do things on our own, or that there is no one to help us. Asking God for help, helps us. It allows us to acknowledge our need for help. It allows us to acknowledge our dependency on God. It allows us to remember God's love and power. It allows us to witness that God is eager to help us.

Question 7. The psalmist suggests throughout the passage that we respond by giving thanks to the Lord for his unfailing love and goodness and wonderful deeds (vv. 1, 15, 21, 31, 43). It also suggests that we exalt and praise God in the presence of others, telling of what God has done for us (vv. 2-3, 22, 32).

Question 8. The wisdom that the psalm offers is multilayered. We see that there are consequences to our actions and sometimes our suffering is brought on ourselves. We see that even when this is the case, God is eager to help us and forgive us and deliver us. We see that many situations we find ourselves in are not because of our doing. We see that whatever situation we find ourselves in, God is willing and able to help. We see that we need to ask for help, and that when we do, we can be confident that God will help us.

Question 9. Reflect on the great love of God for you. If you are in a group, writing individually about your thoughts and feelings in response to God's love and to God's help may be useful before talking about the question together.

Study 4. Confidence in God's Care for Me. Psalm 16.
Purpose: To be encouraged to place our confidence in God's care for us.

Question 2. Go ahead and consider/discuss this question before you read the passage. Imagine a safe place. A secret hiding place. A place in nature where one can be alone. A fortress which locks on the inside.

If you are leading a group, have participants share whatever image of a safe place comes to mind. Then have them think of God as being that kind of safe refuge. Have them think of God as a place to find comfort and protection and safe keeping.

Question 3. The joy that comes from knowing that the Lord is God is being contrast with the sorrow that comes from running after gods who are not God.

Question 4. The purpose of this question is to help you struggle with and integrate the truths of the text more fully. The gifts of care from God which the psalmist names include: provision of food ("portion," v. 5), drink ("cup," v. 5), home ("lot," v. 5, "pleasant places," v. 6), "inheritance" (v. 6), counsel (v. 7), relationship ("at my right hand," v. 8), security and confidence ("I will not be shaken," v. 8, "my body also will rest secure," v. 9), life (vv. 10-11), "joy" (v. 11), and "eternal pleasures" (v. 11).

Question 5. The psalmist responds with acknowledgment, gladness of heart, a rejoicing tongue, and an ability to rest securely (confidence). Take this list and write a sentence, personalizing God's relationship with you as described in this passage. It might read something like: God made me, he saved me, he loves me, he is full of grace toward me, he is powerful to help me, he brought me into life, and he has good things for me to do.

Question 6. If you are leading a group, encourage members to write as many gifts of care they can think of in a limited time (3-5 minutes) and then to share as many of these with each other as they desire.

Question 8. Fears and doubts which hamper confidence in God's care need to be explored without dismissing or minimizing them. Times of difficulty and hardship can leave us with fears that God does not care about us. The people who experienced the trauma of the earthquake in this story, for instance, may feel shaken in their confidence in God's care. Pray for each other at the end of your time together in relation to these fears and doubts.

Question 9. Explore what has helped you in the past to experience confidence in God's care for you. Remembering these things and hearing from others in a group might in itself restore or build new confidence.

Study 5. Confidence in God's Work in My Life. Psalm 25.

Purpose: To grow in confidence in God's work in our lives.

Question 2. Reflect on what it means in practical terms to put your trust in God. Some may say it means asking for help and wisdom for their day. Some may say they seek God for the many decisions of life. Some may say it has to do with remembering that God is always with them. Some may say it has to do with asking God to work in their lives and with recognizing God's work in their lives on a daily basis.

Question 3. The psalmist's requests include: "do not let me be put to shame" (v. 2), "show me your ways" and "teach me your paths" (v. 4), "guide me in your truth and teach me" (v. 5), "remember . . . your great mercy and love" (v. 6), "remember not the sins of my youth and my rebellious ways" and "according to your love remember me" (v. 7).

Question 4. The psalmist appeals to God's love and mercy and goodness as he asks God to work in his life.

Question 5. The psalmist says God works in our lives in many ways: "he instructs sinners in his ways" (v. 8); "he guides the humble in what is right and teaches them his way" (v. 9); he forgives our sin (v. 11); "he confides in those who fear him," and "he makes his covenant known" (v. 14).

Question 6. He says that his feet are caught in a snare (v. 15); he is "lonely and afflicted" (v. 16); he is increasingly troubled and is in anguish (v. 17); his enemies have increased and hate him fiercely (v. 19).

Question 7. The psalmist asks the following of God: "release my feet from the snare" (v. 15), "turn to me and be gracious to me" (v. 16), "free me from anguish" (v. 17), "look on my affliction and my distress" and "take away all my sins" (v. 18), "guard my life and rescue me," don't let me be "put to shame" (v. 20), "protect me" (v. 21), and "redeem Israel" (v. 22).

Question 8. If you are leading a group, encourage participants to call out one or two of these requests that they would like to make of God at this time.

Question 9. If you are leading a group, allow some time

for people to write or reflect on God's work in their lives in the past. Encourage them to share as freely as they wish. Remind them that it is often when we reflect on God's work in the past that our confidence in his ongoing work in our lives in the present and in the future is increased.

Study 6. Confidence in Who God Made Me to Be. Ephesians 2:1-10.

Purpose: To foster confidence in our identity, based on who God made and gifted us to be.

Question 2. Describe the passage in the first person. This might sound something like the following: "The text tells me that there was a time that I was spiritually dead. But because of God's great love for me, he has given me life in Christ. And he seated me with Christ in the heavenly realms, so that he will be able to show me the incomparable riches of his grace. This text tells me that I am saved. That I am saved by grace, that it is a gift, that it is not something I have to earn. It tells me that I am God's workmanship; I was created in Christ to do good works which God prepared in advance for me to do."

Question 3. Describe your thoughts and feelings in response to this rich text. Focus on how it makes you think and feel about yourself. This might include feelings of being loved and valued. Feelings of being rescued, blessed. Feelings of being called to a special purpose in this world.

Question 4. The question is to help you struggle with and integrate the truths of the text more fully.

Question 5. The text tells us that God's relationship with us is one of love (v. 4), grace (vv. 5, 7-8) and power (v.

6). He saved us (vv. 5, 8). He made us, brought us to life and has good things for us to do (v. 10).

Question 6. The text tells us that God wants to give us life (vv. 5-6), salvation (vv. 5, 8), honor (v. 6), kindness (v. 7), grace (vv. 5, 7-8) and good works to do (v. 10).

Question 7. Our part in all of this is faith. It is trust in God. This includes an acknowledgment that we need God, an acceptance of God's love and grace and provision for us. Our part is also to do the good works that have been prepared for us to do.

Question 8. If you are in a group, you'll find that some may have an idea of this. Others may not have any. Some may feel discouraged by not knowing. What we do know is that whatever the good works are that are prepared for us to do, they will have to do with growing in our love of God and growing in our love of others.

Question 9. This text can literally "blow our minds" in terms of who it says God made us to be. We are his creatures, his workmanship. We are loved by him. We are seated with Christ in heavenly realms so God can show us the riches of his grace and love toward us. We are coworkers with God, participating in acts of love and kindness which he prepared for us to do.

InterVarsity Press Bible Studies by Juanita Ryan

Women of Character Bible Studies
A Woman of Balance
A Woman of Beauty
A Woman of Blessing
A Woman of Confidence

LifeGuide® Bible Studies
Psalms II

Life Recovery Guides by Juanita and Dale Ryan
Recovery: A Lifelong Journey
Recovery from Abuse
Recovery from Addictions
Recovery from Bitterness
Recovery from Broken Relationships
Recovery from Codependency
Recovery from Depression
Recovery from Distorted Images of God
Recovery from Distorted Images of Self
Recovery from Family Dysfunctions
Recovery from Fear
Recovery from Guilt
Recovery from Loss
Recovery from Shame
Recovery from Spiritual Abuse
Recovery from Workaholism

Novels by Linda Shands

Seasons Remembered Series
A Time to Keep
A Time to Embrace
A Time to Search
A Time to Speak